EPHESIANS

REFORMED EXPOSITORY BIBLE STUDIES

A Companion Series to the Reformed Expository Commentaries

Series Editors

Daniel M. Doriani
Iain M. Duguid
Richard D. Phillips
Philip Graham Ryken

1 Samuel: A King after God's Own Heart
Esther & Ruth: The Lord Delivers and Redeems
Daniel: Faith Enduring through Adversity
Matthew: Making Disciples for the Nations (two volumes)
Luke: Knowing for Sure (two volumes)
Galatians: The Gospel of Free Grace
Ephesians: The Glory of Christ in the Life of the Church
Hebrews: Standing Firm in Christ
James: Portrait of a Living Faith

Coming in 2022

Song of Songs: Friendship on Fire
John: The Word Incarnate (two volumes)
Philippians: To Live Is Christ

EPHESIANS

THE GLORY OF CHRIST
IN THE LIFE OF THE CHURCH

A 13-LESSON STUDY

REFORMED EXPOSITORY
BIBLE STUDY

JON NIELSON
and **BRYAN CHAPELL**

P.O. BOX 817 • PHILLIPSBURG • NEW JERSEY 08865-0817

Scripture quotations are from the ESV® Bible (The Holy Bible, English Standard Version®), copyright © 2001 by Crossway, a publishing ministry of Good News Publishers. Used by permission. All rights reserved.

All boxed quotations are taken from Bryan Chapell's *Ephesians* in the Reformed Expository Commentary series. Page numbers in quotations refer to that source.

ISBN: 978-1-62995-835-4 (pbk)
ISBN: 978-1-62995-836-1 (ePub)
ISBN: 978-1-62995-837-8 (Mobi)

Printed in the United States of America

CONTENTS

SERIES INTRODUCTION

Studying the Bible will change your life. This is the consistent witness of Scripture and the experience of people all over the world, in every period of church history.

King David said, "The law of the LORD is perfect, reviving the soul; the testimony of the LORD is sure, making wise the simple; the precepts of the LORD are right, rejoicing the heart; the commandment of the LORD is pure, enlightening the eyes" (Ps. 19:7–8). So anyone who wants to be wiser and happier, and who wants to feel more alive, with a clearer perception of spiritual reality, should study the Scriptures.

Whether we study the Bible alone or with other Christians, it will change us from the inside out. The Reformed Expository Bible Studies provide tools for biblical transformation. Written as a companion to the Reformed Expository Commentary, this series of short books for personal or group study is designed to help people study the Bible for themselves, understand its message, and then apply its truths to daily life.

Each Bible study is introduced by a pastor-scholar who has written a full-length expository commentary on the same book of the Bible. The individual chapters start with the summary of a Bible passage, explaining **The Big Picture** of this portion of God's Word. Then the questions in **Getting Started** introduce one or two of the passage's main themes in ways that connect to life experience. These questions may be especially helpful for group leaders in generating lively conversation.

Understanding the Bible's message starts with seeing what is actually there, which is where **Observing the Text** comes in. Then the Bible study provides a longer and more in-depth set of questions entitled **Understanding the Text**. These questions carefully guide students through the entire passage, verse by verse or section by section.

It is important not to read a Bible passage in isolation, but to see it in the wider context of Scripture. So each Bible study includes two **Bible Connections** questions that invite readers to investigate passages from other places in Scripture—passages that add important background, offer valuable contrasts or comparisons, and especially connect the main passage to the person and work of Jesus Christ.

The next section is one of the most distinctive features of the Reformed Expository Bible Studies. The authors believe that the Bible teaches important doctrines of the Christian faith, and that reading biblical literature is enhanced when we know something about its underlying theology. The questions in **Theology Connections** identify some of these doctrines by bringing the Bible passage into conversation with creeds and confessions from the Reformed tradition, as well as with learned theologians of the church.

Our aim in all of this is to help ordinary Christians apply biblical truth to daily life. **Applying the Text** uses open-ended questions to get people thinking about sins that need to be confessed, attitudes that need to change, and areas of new obedience that need to come alive by the power and influence of the Holy Spirit. Finally, each study ends with a **Prayer Prompt** that invites Bible students to respond to what they are learning with petitions for God's help and words of praise and gratitude.

You will notice boxed quotations throughout the Bible study. These quotations come from one of the volumes in the Reformed Expository Commentary. Although the Bible study can stand alone and includes everything you need for a life-changing encounter with a book of the Bible, it is also intended to serve as a companion to a full commentary on the same biblical book. Reading the full commentary is especially useful for teachers who want to help their students answer the questions in the Bible study at a deeper level, as well as for students who wish to further enrich their own biblical understanding.

The people who worked together to produce this series of Bible studies have prayed that they will engage you more intimately with Scripture, producing the kind of spiritual transformation that only the Bible can bring.

Philip Graham Ryken
Coeditor of the Reformed Expository Commentary series

INTRODUCING EPHESIANS

Paul's epistle to the Ephesians has nourished God's people for centuries because of its soaring articulations of the beauty of the gospel of grace, the glorious purpose of the church of Christ, and the loving call believers have received to practically and obediently apply the gospel in their everyday lives—particularly regarding the way they relate to one another in the unified body of Christ. This study's thirteen lessons will divide this rich letter into manageable chunks that you can dig into while also still moving you through it during the course of one season of church life.

The opening words of this epistle indicate that its **author** is the apostle Paul (1:1), and the author reaffirms his identity midway through the letter (3:1). Critical scholars have sometimes raised questions about the letter's Pauline authorship because its style (especially within its first half) seems more abstract, more corporate, and more repetitive than that of others of his epistles. However, this revisionist thought not only denies the text's own clear statements but also naively assumes that an author cannot adjust his style to suit varied purposes. For example, while many themes and phrases from Paul's letter to the Colossians also appear in Ephesians (which further confirms its Pauline authorship), he writes Ephesians with a grander theme in mind.

Most Pauline Epistles are directed toward the problems or progress of an individual church, which requires them to begin with an initial exposition of doctrinal truths that then drive their later practical instructions. However, most scholars understand that Paul's **main purpose** for Ephesians was to write a general letter to the churches within the vicinity or cultural influence of Ephesus. For this collection of churches that were in a culture antagonistic to the gospel, Paul pens themes so grand that they can still take our breath away—and they often move even the apostle to doxology and prayer.

Paul writes to the Ephesians in the **context** of his own imprisonment—see his mentions of this in 3:1 and 6:20, which are probably referring to his house arrest in Rome from A.D. 60–62 (which is described in Acts 28 and also mentioned in Col. 4:3, 10, 18). This two-year imprisonment comes after another two years of trials and incarceration that have followed his Jewish countrymen's initial arrest of him, in Jerusalem, on trumped-up charges. The circumstances surrounding his arrest and appeal to Caesar have kept him from personally nurturing the fledgling churches that have hatched from his missionary journeys. Yet, despite four years of being in bonds, Paul's vision has never been freer and more expansive. He writes with the enthusiasm of a father, and the vision of a prophet, in order to inspire the infant churches he has been forced to love from afar.

Instead of following the normal **pattern** of his epistles, in which he introduces doctrinal development that is then directed at individual problems, Paul immediately moves in Ephesians from a personal salutation to a sweeping explanation of God's eternal plan of salvation. He says that God predestined his love for the Ephesians before the creation of the world and will bring his purposes for his covenant people to culmination through the church's transformation of the world (chapter 1). God's eternal plan and sovereign power include and unite all races, bring the entire world under the reign of Christ through the ministry of the church, and will so definitely come to pass that they have already secured believers' position with Christ in heaven (chapters 1 and 2). Paul presents them running to the past and future horizons of eternity, bridging earth and heaven, leveling all human barriers, transcending all human effort, and giving heavenly origin and purpose to differing gifts within the church—and yet also being driven by such an intimate love that they compel unity, mercy, and purity in the church (chapters 1 through 4). Ultimately he not only assures believers of a transformed world, a place in heaven, and a purpose on earth but also tells them how to have their lives and homes indwelt by the Spirit (chapters 5 and 6). Finally he assures them of the power that the resurrected Christ has made available for the defeat of Satan (chapter 6).

The practical instructions in the second half of the epistle are reminiscent of other Pauline epistles; but, given the grandeur of his opening subjects, the majesty and intimacy of the God he describes, and the hope that these themes provide in the midst of the apostle's own peril, we should not wonder at the fact that his mind and heart often fill with doxology and prayer. This epistle is rightly referenced as a key way to establish the truths of God's sovereignty in our personal salvation. However, when we lift our eyes beyond our personal borders to share even a glimpse of Paul's expansive vision, then we, too, will join his doxology about God's amazing grace—a grace that saves individuals, empowers the church, and, through both, transforms the world.

While certainly all of Scripture should be studied together by God's people, the epistle to the Ephesians will be readily and immediately applicable to the context of believers who are in the local church. Ephesians calls God's people to remember the magnificence of his eternal, sovereign plan for salvation through the work of his Son. It invites us to ponder the grace of God, which reconciles rebellious sinners vertically with their holy God even as it reconciles them horizontally with one another, despite their worldly distinctions and differences. This letter challenges and convicts us through its practical calls to unity, holiness, obedience, and love—and all within a doxological framework of praise and honor to the sovereign and redeeming God. We invite you to undertake this study for the nourishment of your soul and for the health of the body of Christ!

OUTLINE

The spiritual blessings that are given to believers through the eternal plan of the Father, Son, and Holy Spirit (1:1–14)

The transforming power that Christ's authority over all has made available to believers for the fulfillment of God's eternal plan (1:15–23)

God's gracious work of transforming believers from death to life in order to fulfill his eternal plan (2:1–10)

God's gracious work of uniting believers into one body for the fulfillment of his plan (2:11–22)

God's gracious work of including believers from all nations in a corporate mission for the fulfillment of his plan (3:1–13)

God's gracious work, which he performs out of the expanse of his love, of empowering believers to take part in his mission by faith (3:14–21)

God's gracious work of growing believers into one body that has different gifts by equipping them through his love (4:1–16)

God's call for those in Christ's body to walk in ways that are consistent with Christ's love (4:17–32)

God's general instruction regarding how believers are to walk in ways that are consistent with Christ's love (5:1–14)

God's household instruction regarding how believers are to walk in ways that are consistent with Christ's love (5:15–6:9)

God's provisions that enable all believers to fight against Satan's challenges to walking in Christ's ways (6:10–20)

Apostolic greetings that assure believers of the peace and love that have been made available by God's grace in Christ (6:21–24)

Bryan Chapell
Author of *Ephesians* (REC)

LESSON 1

THE FATHER'S PURPOSE

Ephesians 1:1–6

THE BIG PICTURE

As you begin your study of Paul's letter to the Ephesians, you ought to prepare your heart to be captured anew by the sovereignty our great God has displayed through your salvation, in the church of Jesus Christ, and throughout all creation into eternity. This is a glorious epistle—as well as one that has blessed the church of God for centuries.

In this lesson, you will study Paul's brief introduction to the letter, in which he introduces himself as an apostle and identifies his audience: the "saints" in Ephesus who are "faithful" in Jesus Christ (1:1–2). Then he moves quickly toward exulting in the "blessing" of God the Father, which Christians have been given as the recipients of his sovereign election for eternal salvation (1:3–6). And God's sovereign purpose for believers makes Paul truly exultant with praise: he chooses us and predestines us to receive eternal blessing through Jesus. Believers in Jesus have "every spiritual blessing" in the heavenly places (1:3), and God's purpose is to make them "holy and blameless before him" (1:4). His salvation is intimate and loving; we are adopted as his children through faith in Jesus Christ (1:5). God our Father has done all this through the work of the "Beloved"—Jesus the Son, who died and rose for his adopted children (1:6). These beautiful opening verses remind these first-century Christians—and us—of the eternal purpose the Father has for us as he brings us salvation. He planned it—and it is all by his grace and all for the eternal joy and blessing we will receive in him!

Read Ephesians 1:1–6.

GETTING STARTED

1. Why is it good to be reminded—at least sometimes—of who you *were* before you repented and put your faith in Jesus Christ? How can being reminded of our sin and rebellion cause us to praise God and worship him more joyfully for his gracious salvation and forgiveness?

2. Have you witnessed, or been involved in, debates about God's election, sovereignty, or predestination? What has been frustrating about those debates or arguments? How do those who question God's sovereignty in salvation sometimes unfairly portray him—and human beings?

Paul's Expansive Vision, pg. xvi
This epistle is rightly referenced as key for establishing the truths of God's sovereignty in our personal salvation. However, when we lift our eyes beyond personal borders to share even a glimpse of Paul's expansive vision, then we, too, will join his doxology for God's amazing grace that saves individuals, empowers the church, and through both, transforms the world.

OBSERVING THE TEXT

3. What do you notice about the way Paul introduces himself? Glance at two or three of the introductions from his other epistles. What is similar—and what is different—about the greeting and introduction he includes here?

4. Do you notice any repeated words or themes that Paul uses in Ephesians 1:3–6? What are they? What hints might they give about what he wants the Ephesians to understand about God—and about the salvation they have in him?

5. How does Paul point in these opening verses to the sovereign plan of God for the salvation of his people? In what different ways does he talk about this theological reality?

UNDERSTANDING THE TEXT

6. What might be the reason that Paul (here as well as in other epistles) reminds his audience of the role he holds as an "apostle of Christ Jesus" (1:1)? What does that phrase signify about the calling and authority he has been given—why, and how, does Paul say he was called to this role?

7. In what way might Paul's greeting—both the title he gives for himself and the words of blessing his greeting contains (1:1–2)—have been deeply encouraging to the Ephesian believers? What would encourage *you* if the apostle Paul began a letter to you with these words?

8. What might be the reason that Paul uses the words *blessing* and *blessed* (twice) in verse 3? What spiritual blessings has God blessed us with in Christ? In what sense do we share in "heavenly" blessings, even now, as followers of Jesus on earth?

9. What is God's goal and purpose for us, according to verse 4? Why is it incredibly good news that he wants to make us "holy and blameless" before him? How does God the Father ultimately accomplish this?

10. Why is the word *predestined*, which we see in verse 5, sometimes a difficult word for Christians to understand and accept? Why is God's predestination beautiful and wonderful news, according to Paul? How does the picture of adoption help you to more fully understand the unconditional grace and acceptance God has shown you in Christ?

11. What is the end goal of God's salvation of his people (1:6)? As we see in that same verse, who brings about God's great, saving blessing for his people? How does the title "Beloved" add to your understanding of God the Father and God the Son?

We Are in Heaven with God, pg. 21

Because we are in union with Christ, who is in heaven, then we are in heaven with God. The apostle urges praise for God not so much because the Father is in heaven blessing us, as because we are there with him being blessed by him. . . . In our union with Christ, we are already partakers of this spiritual reality, even though it is not fully realized until we are in our glorified state.

BIBLE CONNECTIONS

12. Read Acts 9:1–6. Why is it so important to remember what Paul was like *before* his conversion and his apostolic call? How can remembering this encourage our own hearts and remind us of the grace God has shown to us in Jesus?

13. In Romans 8:15–17, Paul writes about the wonder of the "adoption" that has made Christians into sons and daughters of God. Read those verses now. What benefits come with adoption into God's family, according to the apostle Paul?

THEOLOGY CONNECTIONS

14. The Westminster Confession of Faith describes the blessing of our adoption with these beautiful words: "All those that are justified God vouchsafeth, in and for his only Son Jesus Christ, to make partakers of the grace of adoption; by which they are taken into the number, and enjoy the liberties and privileges of the children of God; have his name put upon them; receive the Spirit of adoption; have access to the throne of grace with boldness; are enabled to cry, Abba, Father" (12.1). Why is this doctrine such good news—and one that is worthy of Paul's repeated use of the word "blessing" as he describes the status we hold as God's redeemed children?

15. The great theologian J. I. Packer writes, "If you want to judge how well a person understands Christianity, find out how much he makes of the thought of being God's child, and having God as his Father."[1] Do you agree with this statement? In what way does Ephesians 1:3–6 support Packer's assertion?

APPLYING THE TEXT

16. Paul refers to the Ephesian believers as "saints" and as "faithful" followers of Jesus Christ. Would you feel comfortable using those titles to describe yourself? Why—or why not? How might the reality of the grace God has shown to you in Jesus enable you to embrace those titles?

17. If we really grasp the truths that this passage is teaching, our necessary response is one of *praise*. Do you regularly sense your heart rising up in praise to God because of the eternal blessing of his salvation, forgiveness, and adoption? If not, why not?

1. J. I. Packer, *Knowing God* (1973; repr. Downers Grove, IL: 1993), 201, quoting an earlier article by Packer in *Evangelical Magazine* 7, pp. 19–20.

18. Why should the reality that God is your Father be an encouragement to you—both now and for eternity? How can you more actively remind yourself that God is not only your Lord but also your Father? Why might we tend to forget this glorious reality?

PRAYER PROMPT

As you conclude your study of this first passage in Paul's letter to the Ephesians, remember that your faith in Jesus Christ is not accidental or meaningless. It is part of God's eternal, gracious, and glorious plan for you; it is your heavenly Father's calling. Today, praise God for seeing fit, in his grace, to call you to repentance from your sin and to faith in his Son. Glorify him for not only forgiving you but also giving you the eternal blessing of adopting you as his child. Finally, pray that you would better understand and know the heavenly blessing that you have, even now, because of your union with Christ by faith!

Praising Our Father, pg. 19
Praise of our Father is really the focus of this passage. The apostle says that we should praise God, because he blesses us as *our* Father.

LESSON 2

THE SON'S MISSION AND THE SPIRIT'S ASSURANCE

Ephesians 1:7–14

THE BIG PICTURE

As we saw in our last lesson, Paul's letter to the Ephesians begins with a worshipful summary of the *calling* that Christians have received from God the Father. We are chosen to be God's children according to the Father's purpose; we are adopted into his family and blessed beyond measure through faith in his Son. In this lesson, Paul's introduction to his letter continues, and we'll see that it is *Trinitarian* in its focus. Christians are called by God the Father, saved by the mission of God the Son, and assured of an eternal inheritance through the ministry and presence of God the Holy Spirit. Paul praises each person of the Godhead in verses 3, 6, and 13.

With regard to the mission of the Son, Paul recounts the saving benefits that Christians receive through the work the Son has done on their behalf (1:7–12). Christ offers us redemption, remission of sins, and the lavish gift of his grace (vv. 7–8). And, more than this, he gives his people the gift of revelation, as they come to understand the mystery of God's will for his people—and for all creation (vv. 9–10). In Christ, God's people come to possess a beautiful inheritance, and the Son is glorified by their doing so (vv. 11–12).

Paul concludes this passage by pointing to the role of God the Holy Spirit, who both "seal[s]" Christians as they believe in Jesus and also serves as the "guarantee" of the inheritance they will receive in Christ (1:13–14). So, as the Ephesians consider their calling and the salvation they have received by faith, Paul longs for them to give praise to the Trinitarian God who ordained this salvation, brought it about, and seals it to their hearts.

Read Ephesians 1:7–14.

GETTING STARTED

1. In what ways are Christians sometimes guilty of minimizing and over-simplifying God's salvation of sinners? What reductionistic pictures or definitions of salvation have you heard being taught?

2. Do you think often about the work that God the Holy Spirit is performing in your life and heart? What might be the reason that many Christians neglect the role of the Holy Spirit when they consider the salvation and spiritual life they have received?

Gripped by God's Mercy, pg. 43
What truth should we take from these verses? We should now have a keen awareness of the redemption, remission, and revelation that are ours solely by the grace of God. Further, we should be so gripped by God's mercy toward us that we will delight to be proclaimers of his grace.

OBSERVING THE TEXT

3. Begin today by thinking back to Paul's words about the eternal purpose that God the Father has for our salvation (1:3–6). What does the doctrine of election remind us about our salvation? How does remembering God's sovereignty in our salvation shake us from a dependence on our good works in order to earn his favor?

4. What are some of the specific saving benefits that Christ brings to God's children, according to Ephesians 1:7–12? How can these verses help to expand your view of the saving work that God has done in your life through Christ?

5. In what way is God the Holy Spirit active in the lives of believers, according to 1:13–14? What unique role does the Holy Spirit play in the lives of those who belong to Christ?

UNDERSTANDING THE TEXT

6. What is the significance of the specific words that Paul uses in the beginning and middle of 1:7? What does "redemption" refer to, specifically? In what way does "the forgiveness of our trespasses" describe an aspect of what Jesus has accomplished for God's people through his death that is slightly different from redemption?

7. How does Paul emphasize, in the rest of that verse through verse 8, the massive outpouring of God's grace on us? Why are words like "riches" and "lavished" important for us to remember as we think about our salvation by grace?

8. What is the "mystery" of God's will, which he makes known to us in Jesus Christ (1:9–10)? How does verse 10 help to explain the ultimate purpose God has, in relation to Christ, for all things on heaven and earth?

The Fruit of Humility, pg. 40

The humility we experience in the light of the mystery of Christ produces additional fruit for his glory. By our humility we gain further insight into who is really in charge of all things. Thus, Paul speaks not only of God's reclamation and revelation, but also of his rule as a way of eliciting our praise for his grace.

9. What term does Paul use at the beginning of 1:11 to describe what is *ahead* for Christians—and how does this serve as a helpful picture for us? Later in the verse, what word does he use to refer to God's sovereign purpose behind our salvation?

10. What is the significance of the fact that Christians are "sealed" with the Holy Spirit when they hear the Word of God and believe the gospel (1:13)? How would you explain this fact to someone who is struggling to understand how God the Holy Spirit is active in our salvation?

11. In what sense is the Holy Spirit our "guarantee" of the inheritance that lies ahead for us in Jesus Christ? How could the hope of this guarantee impact the everyday lives we live as followers of Jesus Christ?

BIBLE CONNECTIONS

12. Paul uses the language of "mystery" here in 1:9—language that he will return to, in more detail, in Ephesians 3. Take a moment to glance ahead at Ephesians 3:1–6. What aspects of the "mystery" of God's will does God reveal through Jesus Christ and his gospel?

13. Read Colossians 1:12 and 3:24—two other instances when the apostle Paul mentions the future "inheritance" that believers possess in Christ. How do these verses expand our understanding of the inheritance that Paul is talking about here in Ephesians? How can these reminders of our future inheritance serve us and help us now, as we live for Christ on earth?

THEOLOGY CONNECTIONS

14. While Christians often talk of the forgiveness of sins they have received through Christ's death on the cross, his death also secured our *redemption*—a word that carries a nuanced meaning: it refers to a *buying back* of something or someone through the *payment of a debt.* Why is it helpful for us to think of Jesus's work on the cross as having provided both our forgiveness *and* our redemption?

15. The Westminster Shorter Catechism tells us, in answer 29, that we are "made partakers of the redemption purchased by Christ by the effectual application of it to us by His Holy Spirit." How does this language help us to further understand how the Holy Spirit "seals" us when we hear God's Word and believe the gospel of Jesus Christ?

APPLYING THE TEXT

16. Paul is clear that every aspect of this salvation that has been accomplished by the Trinitarian God is meant to result in "the praise of his glory" (1:14). Do you often erupt in praise of the glory of God that is revealed through his gracious salvation of you? If not, why not—and how might you change this?

17. In what ways could you continue to grow in your understanding of the "mystery of his will" that Paul mentions in 1:9–10? What role could the study of Scripture, prayer, and involvement in your local church have in this growth?

18. Why is it important for you not to forget the Holy Spirit's role in your coming to faith in Jesus? How can you more intentionally remember and consider this function that the Holy Spirit serves as the "guarantee" of your inheritance in Christ? What applications should it have on your life when you do so?

Included in God's Plan, pg. 58
The weakest of vessels and the vilest of sinners are part of this eternal plan, as are all who believe in him. How do you know that you are included? Because you believe in him and, having believed, you have the testimony of his Spirit in your heart that he is able to bring all things together for his glory and your good.

PRAYER PROMPT

As you consider the mission that the Son undertook for your salvation, and the assurance that the Spirit provides of your ongoing walk with God, spend some time praising your Lord and Savior for the calling you've received as a child of God! Thank Jesus, the Son, for redemption, forgiveness, and the revelation of God's will and purpose. Thank God the Spirit for sealing you in faith—and for serving as an indwelling "guarantee" of your eternal inheritance. Pray that God would fill you with assurance, hope, and joy in him today . . . and praise him for his sovereign work of saving and adopting you as his own.

LESSON 3

THE CHURCH TRIUMPHANT

Ephesians 1:15–23

THE BIG PICTURE

Following the theologically rich, Trinitarian opening of his epistle, Paul now turns to the subject of his *prayers* for the church of Jesus Christ at Ephesus. His prayers for the Ephesians are full of thanksgiving as he recognizes their faith in Jesus and their love for God and one another (1:15–16). He also asks God to give the Ephesian believers a great gift: ongoing spiritual insight (1:17–19). Specifically, Paul longs for these Christians to grasp the beauty and magnificence of the hope they have in Jesus, which guarantees them a "glorious inheritance" along with the presence of God's immense "power" in their lives as they follow him (vv. 18–19). As Paul's lengthy sentence develops, he expands on the glorious power of the resurrected Jesus Christ, who is reigning at the right hand of God the Father in heaven (1:20–21). Amazingly, this Jesus is the "head" of the church, which is identified as his "body" (1:22–23).

This passage gives us Paul's exalted vision for the church of Jesus Christ. Imperfect though his church may be, she is God's perfect plan for declaring the wisdom of his gospel to the world he has made. Members of the church of Jesus Christ must cling to their glorious heavenly future as they joyfully proclaim their Savior to the world in the present.

Read Ephesians 1:15–23.

GETTING STARTED

1. In what ways have you heard people "bash" the church recently? What common criticisms, or stereotypical complaints, do you hear about the Christian church through news outlets or social media?

2. What kinds of prayers do you tend to pray for fellow believers in your church or group of friends? What might sometimes be lacking in those prayers?

OBSERVING THE TEXT

3. As you first read through this passage, what do you see that seems to encourage Paul as he considers the faith and lives of the Ephesian believers? What fills him with joy and thanksgiving?

A Blueprint for Local Church Ministry, pg. 73
The church is God's instrument for world transformation and renewal. . . . [Paul's] following words do not frame a political, marketing, or military strategy but, rather, are a blueprint for the ministry of local churches that will produce mutual love and personal purity so that believers are prepared for godly service in every dimension of their lives.

4. What main things regarding the Ephesian Christians does Paul pray about? Are you surprised by anything that he prays for? What kinds of things does he *not* mention as he describes his prayers for the church?

5. How does Paul point us to the glory of the exalted Christ in this passage? In what ways does he encourage Christians to understand the power and the eternal future that belong to them in Christ?

UNDERSTANDING THE TEXT

6. What main evidences of the Ephesians' spiritual health does Paul mention (1:15)? How does he describe the frequency and nature of the prayers he offers for these believers (1:16)?

7. What makes it obvious that Paul is encouraged by the faith of the Ephesians? What can we learn from the words of thanksgiving he offers regarding the faith of these Christians who still have much room to grow and mature?

8. What kind of knowledge does Paul pray will increase in the Ephesian believers (1:17)? What specifically does he want these Christians to understand about the blessings they have in Christ (1:18)?

9. Paul mentions the "power" of God that is toward those who believe (1:19). What is this power meant to accomplish in the lives of believers? How has God already clearly demonstrated this immense power (1:20)?

10. In what ways does Paul point to the deity, glory, and power of Jesus Christ in verse 21 and the first half of 22? What does Jesus's reign look like currently—and how will his rule and reign be demonstrated in the future?

Perfection in Process, pg. 62

By giving thanks for the good in others he knows to be imperfect, Paul indicates that, with his eyes of faith, he sees them robed in Christ's righteousness. Further, he is giving us wonderful pastoral instruction on how we can offer spiritual support to God's people. We give thanks for the fruit of the Spirit that we can see, even when we know that it has yet to ripen.

11. In what way does Jesus Christ relate to the church, according to the rest of verse 22 into 23? What metaphor does Paul employ to show the relationship that Jesus shares with the church on earth? How do these verses expand your vision of the church's importance and its strategic place in God's plan?

BIBLE CONNECTIONS

12. The prayers Paul offers for the early church provide key glimpses into God's hopes and desires for his people as they grow in faith. Read Philippians 1:9–11, which records Paul's prayer for the church at Philippi. What themes within that prayer are similar to those that you see in this prayer in Ephesians 1? What additional requests does Paul offer to God in that prayer?

13. Our passage for this lesson describes Christ as being the "head" of the church, which is his "body." Read Colossians 1:18–20, which also applies this phrasing to Christ and the church. What language does Paul use as he beautifully describes the saving work that Christ has done for the church? In what ways does this salvation have global implications?

THEOLOGY CONNECTIONS

14. The Scots Confession speaks of the great calling and benefits that are
    for God's people, the church: "It is therefore called the communion,
    not of profane persons, but of saints, who, as citizens of the heavenly
    Jerusalem, have the fruit of inestimable benefits, one God, one Lord
    Jesus, one faith, and one baptism" (chapter 16). How does this quote
    help to further explain the great "inheritance" that belongs to us as
    God's people (Eph. 1:18)?

15. The Westminster Confession of Faith affirms that even the best churches
    on earth are not perfect but are "subject both to mixture and error"
    (25.5). Why should this reality keep us humble as we, the church of
    Christ, seek evermore to grow in purity and holiness? What should it
    teach us about the grace Jesus shows to his still-imperfect people?

APPLYING THE TEXT

16. Paul's words of thanksgiving for the Ephesians' faith and love would
    have certainly encouraged these early believers. What encouragement
    can you draw, today, from these words that he gave to men and women
    who still had much room to grow in their faith?

17. How should the content of Paul's prayer for the Ephesians shape your own spiritual goals? What seems most important to Paul as he prays for these believers—and how can the answer shape your understanding of spiritual growth and maturity?

18. Why should you cherish the church, according to this passage? Why should this lesson's passage make you less cynical about God's people—and more grateful for and loving toward them?

PRAYER PROMPT

As you complete your study of the passage from this lesson, praise God for the gracious gift of faith he has offered through Jesus Christ, his Son. Thank him for, by his grace, giving you a love for both him and his people. Then pray for a deepening understanding of the eternal inheritance that you have in Jesus Christ, your Savior. Ask him to help you to better comprehend the glorious richness of the calling you've received in Christ. Finally, pray that your love will deepen for the church—the body of Christ, your Savior.

Hope, Riches, and Power, pg. 76
Our Lord calls us to a good and a great work. May the eyes of our heart be opened to what he is doing in and through us so that we always speak of the hope, the riches, and the power that are the possession of those God calls his own for the glory of Christ Jesus our Savior.

LESSON 4

THE GIFT OF GOD

Ephesians 2:1–10

THE BIG PICTURE

As we saw in the beginning of Paul's epistle, God's sovereign role in our salvation is undeniable. It is God who elects—who predestines and calls his children to himself through Jesus Christ, his Son. He also calls those children to a new way of life—one that is guided by his Word and marked by faithful obedience to him. The passage you will study in this lesson beautifully weds the doctrine of how God's sovereignty features in our salvation to the call we have been given as his people to walk in newness of life.

In Ephesians 2:1–3, Paul presents the problem: that our sinful position, and our resulting sinful behavior, render us spiritually dead and distant from God—and even make us natural enemies of him. The next verses follow this up, though, with the beautiful hope of the gospel: that we who were dead have been "made ... alive" in Christ by the glorious saving power of God (2:4–7). Christians now have a new status—they live in the power of the resurrection life of Jesus Christ, the risen Savior. Finally, as the passage concludes, Paul explains the call that God places on the lives of believers in Christ: we must proclaim and live out the grace of his gospel (2:8–10). God's people, who have been raised from death to life by God's sovereign work through his Son, are saved for "good works" that God has prepared before time for those who love and serve him (v. 10).

Read Ephesians 2:1–10.

GETTING STARTED

1. What evidence do you see, in your culture, from the media, or among your friends, of the prevailing belief today that human beings are basically *good*? How do people who hold to that belief generally explain the *evil* things that humans do?

2. In what ways have you struggled with the tension between God's sovereign role in your salvation and your responsibility to obey God with your words and actions? What forms has that struggle taken in your life?

OBSERVING THE TEXT

3. As you read through this passage initially, what do you find sobering about Paul's words? What do you find to be particularly hopeful in the passage?

Sovereign Gift; Human Calling, pg. 78
The classic text to which we now turn speaks clearly of the sovereign gift of God's love *and* of his call upon our lives. God's sovereign gift and our human calling wonderfully coalesce to bring him glory and to give us purpose.

4. What does Paul emphasize about the human condition in this passage? How does he illustrate the centrality of God's work in the salvation of sinners?

5. What does Paul say about the purpose God has for the lives of his people and the call he has placed on them? In what sense are "good works" connected to our salvation, according to Ephesians 2:8–10?

UNDERSTANDING THE TEXT

6. What do the first two verses of this passage teach us about our natural *status* with regard to sin and our relationship with God? Whom do we naturally follow and serve—whether intentionally or unintentionally?

7. What does Ephesians 2:3 teach us about our sinful actions? What clear connection do these actions have to our status as fallen people, which we saw in verses 1–2?

8. How does Paul describe God's character in Ephesians 2:4? Why does Paul tell us that God chooses to save sinners in the way he does?

9. What specific language does Paul use to describe God's salvation in 2:5–6—and why might he have chosen these specific words? What is the ultimate end, goal, and purpose of our salvation, according to verse 7? Why is this such good news?

10. What does Paul say in Ephesians 2:8 about the means of our salvation? Why is it so important for us, given what he will go on to teach in verse 10, to understand that we are *not* saved by works? Why does this doctrine remind us not to "boast" (v. 9)?

The Only Source of Life, pg. 81
Jesus alone raised Lazarus to life. He alone is the life-giver because Lazarus was dead and totally unable to do anything. Since we are spiritually dead prior to God giving us new life, the spiritual life we have must be his doing and is to his glory alone.

11. In Ephesians 2:10, Paul explains the role that "works" have in our faith. How is it possible for our good works to be part of *God's* powerful work in our lives and hearts? Why, according to this verse, must they follow from our faith in Jesus Christ?

BIBLE CONNECTIONS

12. Read Ezekiel 37:1–10, in which the prophet Ezekiel gives God's people a vivid picture of the spiritual resurrection that is required in order for sinners to be saved. What is this vision meant to teach God's people about their spiritual condition? How does it point them to the new life that will ultimately come through faith in Jesus Christ?

13. James, in his general epistle to the church, declares to Jewish Christians that "faith apart from works is dead" (James 2:26). Based on the teaching of Ephesians 2:10, what support does Paul offer for this declaration by James?

THEOLOGY CONNECTIONS

14. The Reformed tradition's doctrine of *total depravity* is a way of teaching and understanding our sinfulness, fallenness, and utter spiritual bankruptcy before God. We are not as bad as we could possibly be; but every aspect of our humanity has been infected by sin, making us spiritually "dead" before God and unable to choose him by our own strength. How does Ephesians 2:1–3 explain the reality of this doctrine—and in what way do Paul's metaphors and descriptions help to teach us this truth?

15. The doctrine of *regeneration* is also an important truth that can be seen in our passage for this lesson. According to the Westminster Confession of Faith, God regenerates his chosen people by giving them a "new heart" and causing a "new spirit" to be created in them (13.1). How does Ephesians 2:4–7 point to the truth of this doctrine of regeneration—the truth that sinners are brought to life and faith through a kind of spiritual resurrection?

APPLYING THE TEXT

16. Paul's stark description in 2:1–3 of what we all *were* apart from Christ gives us a clear understanding of how completely we need God's grace and resurrection power in order to be saved. How should these verses

humble you? What should they help you to understand about the spiritual state of your neighbors and friends who do not know Christ?

17. What about Ephesians 2:4–7 should cause you to praise God more joyfully and to wonder at his salvation? What do those verses teach you about the way in which your salvation from sin and death reveals God's *power*—and why is that encouraging?

18. How should Ephesians 2:8–10 motivate you in the areas of obedience, outreach, and acts of love and mercy toward your neighbors? With what attitude, and with what motivation, should you engage in such acts of obedience and love?

A Glorious Purpose, pg. 90

There need be no aloof sitting on the sidelines waiting for God to work because of his sovereignty and our finitude. He has already told us that he has prepared us for good works and, then, in this same passage describes what is good to him: making known his kindness to a world that must glorify him. This is not because God needs us to do so, but because he has so ordained to use us for such a glorious purpose.

PRAYER PROMPT

As you close your study of this remarkable passage in prayer, begin by considering your natural fallen state: that you were apart from God and dead in your sins—unable to choose him. Praise him for making you come alive, by his glorious grace and purpose, to faith in Jesus Christ. That is God's work—not yours! Then thank him for the call that he has graciously placed on your life now that you are a follower of Jesus. Ask him for the strength to proclaim and demonstrate the grace and mercy of the gospel to a world that is desperately in need of God's love, forgiveness, and joy.

LESSON 5

BROUGHT NEAR

Ephesians 2:11-22

THE BIG PICTURE

Throughout the ten remarkable verses of Scripture that we studied in the previous lesson (Eph. 2:1–10), the apostle Paul has called the Ephesian Christians to remember who they used to be apart from Christ (vv. 1–3)— as well as who they are now in Christ (vv. 4–10). Christians have gone from being enemies of God, who are "dead" in sin, to being living servants of God who walk in obedience—and have a glorified and exalted eternal future ahead of them.

Now, in verses 11–22, Paul's focus becomes more horizontal—he again calls the Ephesian believers to "remember"; but this time, what they are to remember is the status they previously held with regard to the covenant people of God: the Jews. He calls this predominantly Gentile group of Christians to remember that, at one time, they stood outside the covenant family of God and were alienated from his promises (2:11–12). Now, however, Gentile believers have been brought near to God through the blood of his son Jesus Christ (2:13). This work of God also gives them a radical new relationship with their Jewish brothers and sisters in Christ—the gospel has broken down the barriers that previously existed between Jew and Gentile (2:14–18). In place of the previous brokenness and alienation, God's people, both Jew and Gentile, are now part of the same "household" of God—one that is being built up as a dwelling place for the Spirit and strengthened by the grace of the God who saves sinners from all nations, languages, and ethnicities (2:19–22). The gospel of God brings sinners into peace with him . . . and also with one another.

Read Ephesians 2:11–22.

GETTING STARTED

1. What evidence do you see in the church today—or perhaps in your own life and heart—that many people's expressions of faith in Jesus Christ are overly privatized or *solely* personal? Why might we sometimes tend toward keeping our faith private rather than sharing openly and vulnerably with others in our local church communities? What are we missing when we privatize our faith to an extreme degree?

2. In what situations, and for what reasons, do you tend to experience tension and discord with other believers in Jesus? What kinds of things tend to cause hostility between believers when it occurs?

Peace with God and All People, pg. 119
Somehow, deep within all believers there is the understanding that peace between the races and with God comes when, through the sacrifice of Christ, we see ourselves as a child in the lap of our heavenly Father and also see other children . . . held with us in his arms.

OBSERVING THE TEXT

3. How would Paul's opening verses in this passage have helped these Gentile, Ephesian Christians to consider—perhaps painfully—what their situation had been when they were apart from Christ? What memories might these verses have evoked in the minds of his readers?

4. What word pictures does Paul use throughout this passage to illustrate our alienation from one another (before Christ) and our unity with one another (through Christ)? What makes them powerful pictures and metaphors?

5. How does Paul call both Jews and Gentiles to see themselves in terms of a *corporate identity*, instead of just an individual identity, throughout this passage? Why is it important for Christians to do this—both then and now?

UNDERSTANDING THE TEXT

6. As Paul describes these Gentile believers in 2:11, what human identities does he assign to them—and why might those labels be a source

of pain, alienation, or hurt for them? How does Paul talk about the different types of alienation that are experienced by those outside the covenant family of God (2:12)?

7. According to Paul in 2:13, how have Gentile believers now been brought near to God and to his family?

8. What work does Jesus's death on the cross accomplish in the lives of previously alienated groups of people (2:14–16)? How does Paul explain the implications of Christ's death for Jews and Gentiles together? What metaphors or pictures from these verses are particularly powerful?

Family Identity and Family Understanding, pg. 101
In Christ we are part of the same family despite our pasts and their consequences. Being one in Christ has consequences for our community. This shared identity means that national identity does not take precedence over our identity as Christians. Racial prejudice cannot be justified and must be resisted. And, in contrast, racial identity that leads to a chip-on-the-shoulder judgmentalism toward other believers who have not fully realized their sin must also be swallowed in family understanding.

9. We see in 2:17 that Jesus preaches a message of peace to those who are "far" (Gentiles) and to those who are "near" (Jews). What common gift do *both* groups receive, which gives them equal access to God the Father (2:18)? Why is this gift so significant to an understanding of the fundamental unity and equality that we share, in Christ, with all believers?

10. How might the *new* labels and titles that are given to those who have come to Christ from outside the Jewish community be deeply encouraging to these Gentile believers (2:19–20)? What is the "foundation" of the house they have joined—and who is the "cornerstone" of that house?

11. For what purpose has God brought this diverse people together through their faith in Jesus Christ (2:21–22)? What goal does he have in mind for this family that is now unified in him?

BIBLE CONNECTIONS

12. Read Acts 10:9–29 and note the way God confronted Peter regarding his heart for the Gentiles. What did Peter need to learn? How is that lesson similar to what you have been studying in Ephesians 2:11–22?

13. Revelation 7:9–12 points us ahead to a beautiful day when the multi-ethnic bride of Christ will gather before his throne and sing praises to his name. In what way should these verses shape your expectation of heaven—and eternity? What impact should this vision have on your understanding of what the church of God is like even now?

THEOLOGY CONNECTIONS

14. The Westminster Confession of Faith describes the globally diverse church of Jesus Christ this way: "The visible Church, which is also catholic or universal under the Gospel . . . consists of all those throughout the world that profess the true religion, together with their children; and is the kingdom of the Lord Jesus Christ, the house and family of God" (25.2). Why is it so easy for us to forget these realities about the church of God? What might we do to more actively make sure we remember, as well as pray for and encourage, our brothers and sisters in other parts of the world?

15. A key tenet of Reformed theology is that one overarching "covenant of grace" follows the fall of humanity into sin and death and stretches throughout all of history. This means that Old Testament Israelites were saved by faith—not by keeping the law. Yet growing up in close proximity to the promises and law of God gave Israelites in the Old Testament remarkable advantages. How does all this explain what Paul

says about the position that Gentile believers were in before they came to faith in Christ (2:11–22)?

APPLYING THE TEXT

16. Paul begins this passage by again calling the Ephesian believers to "remember"—to look back and consider where they were before the grace of Christ transformed their lives. Why can it be good for you to consistently do some gospel "remembering"? How could a consideration of who you *were*, apart from Christ, strengthen both your faith and your relationship with other believers?

17. If Jews and Gentiles in the first century could be brought together by the gospel of Jesus Christ, it is not an exaggeration to say that different believers in Jesus from *any* types of backgrounds can be at peace with one another as they worship the same Savior. Where do you see a need for reconciliation between believers of different backgrounds in your immediate context? How might you encourage this reconciliation and be a catalyst for it?

18. In what way could this passage encourage you to pursue deep and meaningful relationships with brothers and sisters in Christ who come from different cultural backgrounds, ethnicities, or social groups? What might it look like for you to take some initial steps in this direction?

PRAYER PROMPT

As you close your study of Ephesians 2:11–22, spend some time thanking God for bringing you into his covenant family through the blood of his Son, Jesus Christ. Most likely you are a "Gentile" by birth—a natural "outsider" to the promises of God—or at least that is how the apostle Paul would have described you from his perspective! Yet you have been brought near to God through faith in Christ, and you now experience the benefits of all the promises he makes to his people. Praise him for this today! Then ask him for the grace to love and value your brothers and sisters in him who come from different nations, languages, ethnicities, and cultures.

The Joy of Uniting in Our Differences, pg. 116

When we believe that putting hostilities to death brings to life the power of God in our experience, then uniting in Christ with those of different races and backgrounds is not a burden. Variations in style of worship and approaches to ministry fill us with excitement. We become anxious to innovate in ways that demonstrate the manifold wisdom of God rather than anxious about changes to traditions that merely comfort us.

LESSON 6

COUNTERFEIT CALLINGS EXPOSED

Ephesians 3:1-13

THE BIG PICTURE

As Ephesians 3 opens, Paul moves his focus to his own calling as an apostle of the Lord Jesus Christ. Formerly a Pharisee and an enemy of the gospel, Paul is now a man captured by the goals of God. His entire life now revolves around the proclamation of the "mystery" of God—a word he repeats three times in the first six verses of the chapter (3:1–6). This mystery is the beautiful reality that he has just explained in 2:11–22—that Gentiles, through faith in Jesus, are fully included in the family and household of God. Paul, the apostle to the Gentiles, now lives to proclaim this glorious gospel mystery of God. He is also now enraptured by God's grace (3:7–13). His calling to apostleship is more than just self-sacrifice and service for others—it is the joyful proclamation of the grace of God that is ours in Jesus Christ. Paul humbly continues to remember the grace God has shown him, considering himself the "very least of all the saints" (v. 8). And he further proclaims the grace that God has shown to the church and through which he intends to make his gospel wisdom known—in the world and even to the "rulers and authorities in the heavenly places" (v. 10). Paul longs for the saints at Ephesus to remember the access they have, through their faith in Jesus, to the glorious presence of God himself (v. 12) so that they may be encouraged anew by the apostolic gospel he has preached to them and that they have believed (v. 13).

Read Ephesians 3:1–13.

GETTING STARTED

1. What sacrifices have you had to make in order to pursue a certain goal, calling, or act of service to others? How did your conviction about the importance of that goal help your willingness to make those sacrifices?

2. When has your *excitement* about something—a movie, book, place, or food—driven you toward *sharing* it with others? What could you do to approach your gospel witness and evangelism the same way?

OBSERVING THE TEXT

3. In what way does Paul subtly remind his audience of his past, and of the immense grace God has shown toward him, as he begins to describe his apostolic calling at the start of this passage?

Your True Call, pg. 135
We can see this calling of Paul—which is not in doubt—as a window God graciously opens for examining the effects of a true call on the life of a believer. Rather than looking for an initial call similar to Paul's, an examination of his call may reveal to us the impressions that a true calling leaves on one's life and heart.

4. What words and phrases that he uses throughout this passage point to the immensity, glory, and power of the gospel message he has been called to proclaim? How do these words and phrases expand your understanding of and amazement at the gospel of Jesus Christ?

5. What does Paul say about the purpose of the church as this passage ends? What makes his descriptions of the church's calling different from the way people today sometimes talk about the church?

UNDERSTANDING THE TEXT

6. How does Paul talk about his imprisonment in 3:1—and what does that tell you about his understanding of God's sovereignty over his life and ministry? We see in 3:2 that he understands his ministry of the gospel of grace to be a matter of "stewardship" for the Gentiles—to be something that God has committed to his care for an intentional purpose. In what way has Paul been a faithful steward (as well as *continuing* to be one, even as this epistle progresses) of the gracious gospel of God for the Ephesian believers?

7. What does Paul affirm about the way in which the mystery of God was revealed to him (3:3–5)? Why is this important for him to explain—and how does it serve to remind the Ephesians of his authentic apostleship?

8. What is the "mystery" of God, according to Paul (3:6)? What about the history of God's people, as recorded in the Old Testament, makes this a mystery? Why is this mystery such good news for the Gentiles?

9. How does Paul demonstrate humility, as well as an ongoing sense of wonder and amazement at his own salvation and calling from God, in Ephesians 3:7–8?

10. What does Paul teach us about the eternal plan of God, which has now been fully revealed in the gospel of Jesus Christ (3:9)?

Enraptured by Grace, Proclaiming Christ, pg. 143
Being enraptured with grace is the nature of Christian calling. Such awe of grace certifies our calling as genuine and energizes it in the face of sacrifice. The truly called are so enraptured by the grace of God toward them that the attacks of others, the difficulties of their circumstances, their lack of worldly comfort, and their lack of recognition in the world do not dissuade them from the joy of proclaiming Christ.

11. What do you learn from Ephesians 3:10–13 about God's purpose for the church? What is surprising to you about the calling the church has been given? In what way could these verses encourage you to better appreciate, and invest in, the work of *your* local church?

BIBLE CONNECTIONS

12. In 1 Timothy 1:15, Paul uses similar language to that of Ephesians 3:8 and calls himself the "foremost" of sinners. What is he trying to emphasize, by using such terms, about the status he has before God apart from Christ? How can we learn from his understanding of the depth of his sin and need?

13. Ephesians 3:12 tells us that as members of the church we have "boldness [before] and access" to God. Read Hebrews 4:14–16. How does the author of Hebrews further expand on the confidence with which we can approach a holy God? What has secured this confidence for us—finally and eternally?

THEOLOGY CONNECTIONS

14. The answer to question 60 of the Heidelberg Catechism reminds us of a beautiful reality: "I have grievously sinned against all the commandments of God and kept none of them, and am still inclined to all evil, yet God, without any merit of mine, of mere grace, grants and imputes to me the perfect satisfaction, righteousness, and holiness of Christ." How does Paul reflect on this glorious gospel truth in the passage you have been studying? Why should this reality encourage and enrapture your heart today?

15. The Westminster Confession of Faith affirms that "Christ hath given the ministry, oracles, and ordinances of God, for the gathering and perfecting of the saints" in the church (25.3). How is this affirmation similar to Paul's teaching in Ephesians 3:10–13 about what God has entrusted to his church?

APPLYING THE TEXT

16. Paul, who was formerly a powerful religious leader, sacrificed immensely in order to become an apostle to the Gentiles of the gospel of Jesus Christ—he went from having a place of prominence to being imprisoned for the sake of the gospel. How should his example encourage

you to willingly accept potential losses of privilege, position, or power for the sake of the gospel of Jesus Christ?

17. If Paul considered himself the "least of all the saints" (3:8), how should we think about ourselves regarding the gracious salvation *we* have received through Jesus Christ? How can Paul's amazement over his gracious calling remind us to be astonished at the grace of God that we see in our lives?

18. In what way should this passage serve as a call to you to engage in gospel witness, both in your capacity as an individual and through your involvement in your local church?

Attributes of Genuine Calling, pg. 148

We learn from Paul's words that our calling has many similar attributes if it is genuine. We—for no merit of our own—are willing to die to self and live for others. We vow to share with others everything that we have in Christ. . . . Why would we do such things? Because we are aware of the watching world, and the heavenly hosts give glory to God when they observe the church exhibiting such grace.

PRAYER PROMPT

The calling that Paul received to proclaim the mystery of the gospel of God should be a reminder for us of how the good news of Jesus has come to us, as well! What a glorious mystery it is that we, who are separated from the Israel of the Old Testament by both centuries and continents, get to share nonetheless, through faith in his Son, in the eternal blessings of God. Today, praise God for the gift of the grace that he offers through Jesus and ask him to make you even more enraptured by his love and mercy. Then ask him to remind you of your own calling to worship and enjoy your Savior—and to make him known to a world in need.

LESSON 7

POWERFUL AND GLORIOUS LOVE

Ephesians 3:14-21

THE BIG PICTURE

As we studied in our last lesson, Paul views his gracious calling from God to be one of proclaiming the mystery of the gospel of Jesus Christ—a gospel that is fully extended to Gentiles who put their faith in him. Now, Paul begins to pray for the Ephesians themselves, who make up the church that has been entrusted with this glorious gospel. His prayer is for them to receive power—not for the purpose of worldly accomplishment but so that they may fully grasp the love that God has shown them through Jesus Christ their Savior (3:14–19). He prays that the Spirit would strengthen the saints at Ephesus to be able to understand the depths of Christ's love, to continue to ever deepen their faith in their Savior, and to be "filled with all the fulness of God" (v. 19). The end goal of this pouring out of God's power on his church is to bring him glory; we next see Paul following his prayer for power with doxological praise (3:20–21). In these final two verses of the passage, he emphasizes that God is "able" to accomplish this wonderful spiritual work in the lives and hearts of the Ephesian believers—and in ways even beyond their thoughts and imagination. In the same way, this passage directs believers today to pray for God's power to increase our faith and understanding, as well as for the gracious assurance that we hope for from God that he will accomplish his good work in the midst of the people he has redeemed through his Son.

Read Ephesians 3:14–21.

GETTING STARTED

1. When people pray for power from God, what do they often mean—and what are they often hoping to accomplish with this power?

2. What kinds of things do people in today's culture tend to think that God wants from them—and *for* them?

OBSERVING THE TEXT

3. How does Paul set up the prayer he offers for the Ephesians in 3:14–16? On what basis does he pray for them?

Ministry Priorities, pg. 151

The apostle Paul uses the truth that what we love motivates and enables our actions to summarize all the doctrine presented thus far in Ephesians. And in uniting spiritual strength to the believers' knowledge of God's love, the apostle tells us what must take priority in ministry that will truly help others discover God's transforming power.

4. What are some of the spiritual qualities whose presence in the lives and hearts of the Ephesians seems to be most important to Paul? What does he want them to know about God's character, his heart, and the intention he has for them?

5. In what ways should Christians be encouraged, throughout this passage, by what Paul both teaches and implies about the character of God and the love he has for his children?

UNDERSTANDING THE TEXT

6. What potential relationship do you see between Ephesians 3:15 and what Paul has previously taught about Jews and Gentiles in terms of their relationship to the household of God (2:11–22)?

7. In what way is God *personally* active in the lives and hearts of believers, according to 3:16? What makes this so encouraging?

8. What does Paul's use of language such as "rooted" and "grounded," in 3:17, imply about what the Spirit seeks to accomplish in the lives of Christians? How might being more "rooted" and "grounded" in our faith in Christ strengthen us against sin and temptation?

9. What exactly does Paul want the saints at Ephesus to "comprehend," according to verse 18 and the first half of 19? What makes the ongoing deepening of this comprehension so important to Christian faith—as well as key evidence that we have rightly understood the gospel of grace?

10. How does 3:19 explain what Paul means by being filled with the "fullness" of God? What do you think is his reason for saying that the love of Christ actually "surpasses" knowledge?

Truths at Soul Depth, pg. 159

You may know all of these basic gospel truths, and the Ephesians knew them; but Paul repeats these essentials because he knows that until they sink to soul depth, we will rely on our own powers of perception and strength to combat sin. And, consequently, we will remain powerless before the assaults of the Evil One.

11. How is Ephesians 3:20 meant to shape our expectations of and hopes for what God will do in our lives and hearts? To what end is he working in his people—both on an individual basis and in the context of the church (3:21)?

BIBLE CONNECTIONS

12. In Philippians 4:19, Paul promises that God will provide for us according to his "riches," just as he prays in Ephesians 3:16. What kinds of riches is Paul alluding to in both places? What types of blessings for God's people is he concerned with?

13. Read Romans 8:38–39. What language does Paul use in those verses that is similar to the language you have been studying from Ephesians 3:18–19? What truths about God's love for his people is he seeking to explain in both places?

THEOLOGY CONNECTIONS

14. The Westminster Larger Catechism teaches in answer 9 that there are three persons in the Godhead, who are "distinguished by their personal properties." How does Ephesians 3:16–17 explain the way in which God

the Holy Spirit and God the Son are "distinguished" by their different roles and properties, even as both persons remain fully God?

15. Paul's doxological conclusion to this section of Ephesians, in verses 20–21, articulates a desire for God to be *glorified* through the church, and through Christ Jesus, for all generations. Why is the central theme and goal of God's *glory* so important for us to remember, value, and pray about?

APPLYING THE TEXT

16. In what ways can this passage help you to push back against faulty understandings of what God's power should look like in the lives of believers? How can it help to shape your understanding of how God's power is at work in the lives of his people—even when they appear weak in the eyes of the world?

God at Work, pg. 173
But how will God apply this sovereign power? The answer to that question will truly stretch our imagination—and our faith. For what the apostle claims is that God will work sovereignly according to his power that is "at work in us." God works in us personally.

17. In what way can this passage shape your prayers—for yourself, for your church, and for believers in Jesus around the world? What about your prayers seems short-sighted, and too *small-minded*, when you compare them to Paul's prayer from this passage?

18. How should these verses that we have studied encourage you—especially during times of spiritual dryness, doubt, and discouragement?

PRAYER PROMPT

The best way to respond in prayer to this passage is to echo Paul's prayers for the Ephesian believers—and for all who belong to Jesus Christ. Pray that God would pour out his power, through his Spirit, on your life and heart in order to help you better grasp the immense love he has shown you in Christ. Ask him to accomplish his good work in you as you place your faith more and more in his Son. Pray that he would remind you that he, your Father, is *able* to do this good work in your life, for his glory and for the good of those around you.

LESSON 8

OWNER'S MANUAL FOR THE CHURCH

Ephesians 4:1-16

THE BIG PICTURE

The beginning of Ephesians 4 marks a major shift in the letter. For three glorious chapters, Paul has been reminding the Ephesian believers of the salvation they have gained through Christ—a salvation that reconciles them both to God and to one another. He has been laying the theological foundation for the lives they are to live as believers who have been brought into God's family through the finished work of Jesus. Now, as chapter 4 begins, Paul will focus more on giving instruction to the church as he guides its members practically and concretely toward a vision for how to live with one another in the body of Christ. The passage that we will study in this lesson looks backward, as well as forward, as Paul provides summaries of the gospel foundation that has been described in the earlier parts of the letter while also preparing to give more practical instruction in the rest of chapter 4 through chapter 6. In short, these sixteen verses give the Ephesian Christians a vision for how to pursue maturity through *unity*. The transformation they have experienced through Christ, and the witness they bear to the world, will be demonstrated through their gentleness with one another, their humility, and their pursuit of unified growth toward Christlikeness in every way. The passage begins with a reminder of the common call that all Christians have received in Christ, which gives them all the same family name, identity, and testimony (4:1-6). Then Paul affirms the differences that exist within the body of Christ despite this common call—differences that are to be celebrated as each member plays his or her part (4:7–14). Finally, he celebrates the dependency that all believers in the body of Christ share—a dependency both on Christ and on one another (4:15–16). This passage calls believers in the body of Christ to be unified in their diversity, as we live humbly and joyfully within the variegated family of God.

Read Ephesians 4:1–16.

GETTING STARTED

1. Describe a time when you were part of a group, team, or staff that had a particularly strong sense of unity and purpose. What factors about that group led to this unity? What would have presented a threat to that sense of togetherness and common purpose?

2. What is it that makes people tend toward belonging to monolithic groups and spending time with people who are exactly like them? Why is it important for us, as Christians, to pursue relationships with people who are *different* from us—and especially so within the body of Christ?

How the Church Must Function, pg. 182

In the opening chapters of Ephesians, Paul has shared his grand vision of the divine power available to the church for spiritual and cultural transformation. But now there is an important shift in focus. In the remaining chapters, Paul pours his efforts into describing how the church purchased by Christ's sacrifice must function in order to fulfill its mission.

OBSERVING THE TEXT

3. What earlier points that Paul has made about the Ephesian believers' calling, salvation, and role in the family of God do you see him looking back to and referencing in this passage?

4. What are some of the main purposes of the church of Jesus Christ that Paul addresses throughout this passage?

5. What, according to this passage, are some of the important ways in which believers are called to relate to one another, and to view each other, within the body of Christ?

UNDERSTANDING THE TEXT

6. In what way could Ephesians 4:1 be read as a kind of purpose statement, or thesis, for the second half of the letter? These final three chapters of Ephesians will go on to present a number of instructions and commands—why is it important to view the gospel truths that Ephesians 1–3 contain as being the essential foundation for that material

in Ephesians 4–6? What would be dangerous about seeking to obey those commands without grasping the gospel foundation that underlies them?

7. What attitudes and actions are supposed to characterize relationships among the people of God (4:2–6)? What foundational truths are believers to keep in mind as they relate to one another in the context of the body of Christ?

8. What does 4:7 tell us about the foundation of the gifts we see in the church as well as the variety of those gifts? Where do these gifts come from, ultimately, and how does the work of Christ relate to this (4:8–12)? What must we conclude about the diversity that characterizes both the gifts and the people that we see in the church of God?

The Generosity of Jesus, pg. 190

We gain fresh and tender appreciation of the Savior and those about us when we see that the variety of the gifts is an expression of the great generosity of Jesus. In this variety he is sharing more of himself than can be contained in any one of us. Not any one of us has to do all the work of the kingdom because Christ has not given all of his gifts to any one person.

9. What do 4:13–14 teach us about the goal behind the growth we experience as the people of God? How, according to these verses, can growing in maturity guard us—and against what can it guard us?

10. In what way does 4:15 function as a call for the local church to focus explicitly on Christ? What is the goal of the church, and of every believer, according to this verse?

11. What does 4:16 say about our dependency not only on Christ but also on one another who are in the body of Christ? Why is it so important for every part of a "body" to be working properly—as well as working together? What does this metaphor imply about the way we should think about the church?

BIBLE CONNECTIONS

12. Read 1 Corinthians 12:12–26. How does Paul expand in this passage on the illustration of the church as a "body"? What conclusions must we draw from these verses about the way we should treat *all* people, as well as *all* gifts, that we encounter within the body of Christ?

13. In John 15, Jesus uses the picture of a vine and its branches to illustrate the fundamental dependence that his people, together, have on him. Read John 15:4–5 now. How do these verses complement Paul's teaching from Ephesians 4:15–16?

THEOLOGY CONNECTIONS

14. One of the chief ideas of the Protestant Reformation was the concept of the "priesthood of all believers"—the idea that all Christians have equal access to God through the great High Priest, Jesus Christ. How do you see Ephesians 4:11–12 supporting that concept—specifically in the way it explains the purpose of pastors and teachers and their role in relation to the people of the church?

15. The Westminster Confession of Faith teaches that the ministry of the church, which includes the ordinances that God has given to it, exists "for the gathering and perfecting of the saints" (25.3). What would you say the "perfecting" of believers in the church looks like, according to what you have studied in this lesson (and especially verses 13–16)?

Building Together, pg. 199
Christ makes us one and obligates us to work together so that we can use our different gifts to build his church. In this task, all gifts are needed and everyone must do his or her part. We must never rule ourselves out of the process of building the church that is Christ's transforming power for this earth and for the eternity of multitudes that he is drawing to himself.

APPLYING THE TEXT

16. Why is it important for us to remember the fundamental *sameness* that characterizes all of us who are in the body of Christ? What can you do to actively remind yourself and others of the common call, identity, and witness that all Christians share through their faith in Jesus?

17. What can serve to remind you of the vastly different gifts—and people—that Jesus Christ has given to his church? How can you challenge yourself to spend more time with Christians who are different from you in order to celebrate the fullness and diversity of the body of Christ?

18. What kinds of gifts tend to be celebrated the most in the church today? How could your church, as well as you individually, work to celebrate all kinds of the gifts that God has given to his people in the body of Christ?

PRAYER PROMPT

Today, as you close your study of this passage in Ephesians, begin your prayer by praising God for the unity that you share with all Christians who have been redeemed through the blood of Christ. Ask God to give you the grace to remember and celebrate this fundamental unity you have with his people from all over the world. Then pray that he will give you a growing understanding of and appreciation for the different gifts that Jesus Christ himself has provided to the church. Ask him to help you to celebrate the generous heart of our God, who has not given every gift to every believer but has distributed them throughout a diverse body that works together to glorify him and make his name known.

LESSON 9

THE OLD AND THE NEW

Ephesians 4:17-24

THE BIG PICTURE

As we saw in our previous study, the apostle Paul began the second half of his epistle to the Ephesian Christians by reminding them of the gracious heavenly calling they have received through Christ—one that is shared by each member of the church. Now, in the passage for this next study, Paul contrasts the darkened, futile, and hopeless lives of those who are under sin with the glorious, holy, "new" way of life that exists in Christ. The passage begins with a warning, as Paul reminds the Ephesian Christians that they must no longer walk in the way of the "Gentiles"—his generic term for those who are outside the covenant people of God (4:17–19). To return to such a life of sin would bring darkened minds, hardened hearts, and deadened senses to these Ephesian Christians. Paul's warning is clear: Christians must not turn back to a life of sin—as enticing as it often seems! The apostle then explains the Christian calling they have received, which involves a life of putting sin to death and of being remade, more and more, into the image of Christ (4:20–24). This is a life that's marked by careful *listening* to the Word of God as well as intentional *obedience* to God's commands. The Christian calling involves a "putting off" of the old self and a "putting on" of the new self (vv. 22, 24)—which is intentional on the part of the Christian while also being empowered by the Holy Spirit, who indwells those who have become true children of God through faith in Jesus Christ. This is, then, a passage full of stern warnings as well as kind invitations—God's people are invited to reject sin and to embrace the newness of life that is available through Christ their Savior.

Read Ephesians 4:17–24.

GETTING STARTED

1. Why are bad habits—and especially those that are developed over a long period of time—so difficult to break? And even after they are broken, what kinds of discipline must one practice in order to maintain victory over them and freedom from them?

2. Describe some of the warnings you have received in your life from leaders or mentors whom you respect. What was your initial response to these warnings? How did you ultimately benefit from them?

Putting Off and Putting On, pg. 202

Having told us in preceding verses of the world-transforming and heaven-glorifying mission of the body of Christ, in which members with very different backgrounds and gifts are accepted as each does his or her part, the apostle now begins to discuss how each person will function. This section of his letter is a study in contrasts of what we are to put off and what to put on in order to do our part for the church to fulfill her purposes.

OBSERVING THE TEXT

3. How would you describe the general tone that the apostle Paul uses throughout this passage? What specific language and wording do you see that hint at the intensity and seriousness underlying his warnings and commands?

4. What does Paul obviously assume about the Ephesian Christians to whom he is writing (4:20–21)? How does this assumption shape the call that he gives to them throughout the remainder of the passage (4:22–24)?

5. What is hopeful about this passage, even in the midst of its stern warnings? How does the truth of the gospel of grace shape everything that Paul commands and teaches throughout it?

UNDERSTANDING THE TEXT

6. What makes it clear that 4:17 begins a section of warning for the Ephesian Christians? What is significant about the fact that Paul is issuing this warning to *believers* in Jesus—and what must we conclude from that?

7. What clear effects does sin have on the lives of those who turn to it instead of to Christ (4:18–19)? How can each of these effects lead to the next—and how does this comprehensive picture of the darkness and hopelessness of sin give weight to Paul's warning?

8. What does Ephesians 4:20 confirm about the audience for whom Paul intends the warning that he included in the previous verses? How does he describe the way in which the Ephesians have come to faith in Jesus (4:21)?

9. What decisive action does Paul, in the next verse, call Christians to engage in? How does he describe the "old self"? To what is it linked?

10. What would you say it means for the Ephesian believers to be "renewed in the spirit of [their] minds" (4:23)? How might this renewal act as a contrast with what he described in 4:17?

Motivation, pg. 214

Those in love with the Savior will hear his voice, and it will break their hearts to know that they are hurting him. Christ's love is behind the apostle's warnings. Love for the Savior, regard for him, delight in him, and a desire for us to walk with him motivate all Paul says. That is why the apostle says we should not only put off our old self, but also put on the new self.

11. How does Paul explain the characteristics of the "new self" in 4:24? What might be some ways that a believer in Jesus can "put on" that new self?

BIBLE CONNECTIONS

12. Read Romans 1:28–32. To what, according to these verses, does the dark progression of sin and rebellion lead? How do the descriptions of sin that these verses contain illustrate how darkened and futile sinners' minds are, as we see Paul mentioning in Ephesians 4:17–18?

13. Colossians 3:5–17 is another passage in which Paul uses the language of "putting off" and "putting on." Read those verses now. What specific qualities and actions does he list in that passage—and what do they add to what he has been saying in this lesson's passage from Ephesians?

THEOLOGY CONNECTIONS

14. The Westminster Confession of Faith describes how *sanctification* works in the lives of Christians by explaining that, by the grace of the Holy Spirit, "the dominion of the whole body of sin is destroyed, and the

several lusts thereof are more and more weakened and mortified, and they are more and more quickened and strengthened, in all saving graces, to the practice of true holiness" (13.1). How does this description expand on what Paul is calling the Ephesian believers to do in this passage you have studied?

15. Given that description above of what the Holy Spirit accomplishes in Christians' lives, what role does the passage that you have been studying say that the *Christian* plays in his or her own sanctification? Are we active participants in our sanctification even though God supplies the power for us to be able to change? Why is it important for us to remember both God's power *and* our own active involvement in our sanctification?

APPLYING THE TEXT

16. Even if you have been a Christian for quite some time, the warnings within Scripture are still meant to offer you spiritual exhortation—and to make you vigilant and disciplined regarding your walk with God. How can you best respond to the warnings of Ephesians 4:17–19 after having studied them in this lesson?

17. How can this passage serve to point you back to the fundamental identity of a child of God that is yours through faith in Christ (see 4:20–21)? Why must any attempt to strive for obedience always begin with a gospel reminder?

18. What sins do you feel called to "put off," more and more? In what practical ways could you practice the "putting on" of your new self through the power of the Holy Spirit?

PRAYER PROMPT

Today, ask God to help you to heed the earnest warnings that the apostle Paul has written in this passage. Pray that he would enable you to see more clearly the futile nature of sin—and the dark path of hopelessness to which it leads. Ask your heavenly Father to fill you with hope in your Savior, Jesus Christ, so that you will joyfully set out to "put on the new self" continually as you follow him day by day (4:24). Thank him that the Holy Spirit, who indwells you through your faith in Christ, enables you to put off sin, obey God's Word, and grow in the grace and knowledge of Jesus your Savior!

Made for Life in Christ, pg. 216
The reason that sin does not satisfy is the same reason that salt water does not. We were made for what the Bible calls living water, the truth and life that are in Christ Jesus. Those who are redeemed will find only in him and in the life he designs the health and happiness for which we were made.

LESSON 10

WITNESS OF GRACE

Ephesians 4:25–32

THE BIG PICTURE

As Paul continues this more practical section of his letter, his focus turns to what the life of gospel grace should look like in the context of relationships in the church. Those whose hearts and lives have been changed by Jesus will be marked by truthful speech, gracious forgiveness, and honest labor for the Lord (4:25–28). Christians who have been renewed by Christ reject the temptation of falsehood, as well as bitter anger and vengeful thoughts, as they work diligently for the glory of God and the good of others. These same themes continue throughout the second part of the passage, as Paul again speaks of believers' words, thoughts, and actions (4:29–32). Christians who have been renewed by Jesus Christ guard their tongues, refusing to allow coarse and rude talk to flow from their mouths. Instead, his followers seek to build up and edify their brothers and sisters in the body of Christ and thus speak words of love, encouragement, and joy. At the root of all relationships in the church is the cross of Jesus Christ, at which we see the forgiveness that must shape our own gracious forgiveness of others (v. 32). This passage, then, presents a picture of how the lives Christians live in the church community can be a living evidence of God's grace. Those who are renewed by Jesus bear witness to his grace through their words, thoughts, and actions—all of which has great impact on the lives and souls of the people around us.

Read Ephesians 4:25–32.

GETTING STARTED

1. What are some of the sinful attitudes or habits that seem to result in the most destruction to a group of friends? To a team or club? To a local church? Why do these attitudes or habits have such a damaging effect?

2. Why should the forgiveness of others clearly characterize a person who has truly met Jesus Christ? What makes forgiving others so difficult, in many cases? When have you seen forgiveness serve as a "witness of grace" in your life—or in the life of someone who is close to you?

OBSERVING THE TEXT

3. The two sections of this passage (4:25–28 and 4:29–32) follow a similar pattern. What three general themes does Paul address in both of these sections?

The Grace Secured for Us, pg. 218

We are not to live to secure grace but to live out the grace that he secured for us. And so that we will not simply let such a principle evaporate into abstraction, the apostle now begins to spell out plainly what it means to live as those renewed by his grace in how we speak, think, and act.

4. In what way do these three themes basically encompass the entire
   Christian life? Why are they helpful categories for evaluating the way
   in which Christ is remaking us more and more into his image?

5. What are some ways in which the gospel of Jesus Christ clearly perme-
   ates the commands Paul gives in this passage? What makes it obvious
   that Paul is urging the Ephesians to act in certain ways not in order to
   earn God's favor but rather so that they will bear *witness* to the favor
   and grace of God that is already theirs through their faith in Jesus?

UNDERSTANDING THE TEXT

6. How does 4:25 say that believers should use their words—and what
   kind of talk should they avoid? What truth about the community of
   God's people whom we encounter in the church serves as Paul's foundation for giving this command?

7. What should be the way in which Christians deal with anger, according to what Paul says in 4:26? In what way might we give the devil an
   "opportunity" if we hold on to feelings or thoughts of anger toward
   others (4:27)?

8. How does 4:28 say that the gospel should shape our approach to work? What is at least part of the goal of making money, according to what Paul says in this verse?

9. What kind of talk should those who are renewed by Christ avoid—and why (4:29)? How does Paul describe the God-honoring words that should flow from our mouths? What is the goal of using that kind of speech in the church?

10. What should Christians do to allow the Holy Spirit to purify the thoughts they have about others, according to 4:30–31? What might it look like to "put away" bitterness and malice?

Representing Christ, pg. 226

The significance of the impact of our obedience on others as well as on us keeps Paul writing. Though he has already addressed how what we say, think, and do is not merely about self-promotion before God or self-protection from God, the idea of representing Christ and his grace stimulates greater intensity of expression.

11. Why should the forgiveness that God has shown to us through Jesus Christ shape our response to others when we are wronged (4:32)? How can the tenderhearted forgiveness that we show to others bear witness to the saving work of Jesus? How can a refusal to forgive others damage our gospel witness?

BIBLE CONNECTIONS

12. Read Matthew 15:11–20. How does Jesus's teaching about the revealing nature of our *words* agree with, and give weight to, the commands from Paul in the passage you are studying? How does Jesus say that our speech reveals who we truly are?

13. In his prayer and his teaching in Matthew 6:12–15, Jesus speaks about forgiving others. What makes his words about forgiveness—and especially those in verses 14–15—so convicting for Christians? In what way do they confirm what Paul says to the Ephesian believers in verse 32 of this lesson's passage?

THEOLOGY CONNECTIONS

14. The Westminster Shorter Catechism teaches us in answer 77 what the ninth commandment requires: "the maintaining and promoting of truth between man and man, and of our own and our neighbor's good name, especially in witness-bearing." How does Paul teach this requirement clearly in this lesson's passage (see 4:25, 29)?

15. In his *Institutes of the Christian Religion*, John Calvin explains that our forgiveness of others, which God commands, is not a work that earns us his forgiveness; rather, "by the use of this expression the Lord has been pleased partly to solace the weakness of our faith, using it as a sign to assure us that our sins are as certainly forgiven as we are certainly conscious of having forgiven others" (3.20.45). In what way might forgiving others strengthen your faith—and how could God use such an action to confirm the work he has done in your life and heart?

The Privilege of Forgiving, pg. 232

By the practice of forgiveness we have the privilege of being a living witness to the One we most love, and who has loved us eternally and sacrificially. This is the ultimate motivation that gives us joy in our suffering, strength for obedience, and love for his commands. My life will never deserve his love, but my life can reflect his love; and because I love him, I will live for him in what I say and think and do.

APPLYING THE TEXT

16. In what ways has this passage convicted you regarding your words and your patterns of speech? Are there aspects of your talk or conversation that you need to bring more intentionally under the lordship of Christ, in all purity, honesty, and love? If so, pray about them now.

17. How could being more mindful of the impact that your growth in the area of holiness has on *others* help and motivate your efforts regarding obedience and sanctification?

18. In what situations might God be calling you to fully, freely, and joyfully extend forgiveness today? What sometimes holds you back from forgiving others when they wrong you, and what could you do to better remember the rich forgiveness that God has offered you in Christ?

PRAYER PROMPT

As you close your study of this passage, lay your words, thoughts, and actions before God as you invite the Holy Spirit to renew them all through his ongoing work more and more. Pray for God to give you the grace to see more clearly the encouraging effect that your holiness and obedience can—and will—have on the lives of others who live in community with you. Ask God to help the reality of the gospel, and of the forgiveness he has offered you through Christ, to permeate every relationship that you have—and particularly those that are most difficult.

LESSON 11

IMITATORS OF GOD

Ephesians 5:1–21

THE BIG PICTURE

As Paul continues to offer both commands and words of practical instruction to the Ephesian believers, he begins the next chapter of his letter by again reminding them of the fundamental identity they have as children of God (5:1–2). Christians are "beloved children" of the Father through the work of Christ, who "gave himself up" in their place. This gospel reminder that he issues then gives way to a beautiful outpouring of instructions concerning the Christian life—all of which are summed up in one thematic phrase: "be imitators of God" (v. 1).

Paul first focuses on the issue of sexual purity in the lives of God's people, which is multifaceted in terms of both what it celebrates and what it rejects (5:3–7). God's beloved children are called to avoid sexual sin, as well as all impurity and covetousness, in practice. And not only that, but their words, as well, are to be free from impurity and rudeness (v. 4). God's people must even be cautious and mindful about relationships that would lead them toward sexual sin and impurity, since the power of deception and temptation is so strong (vv. 5–7).

Next, Paul calls the Ephesian believers to understand their role as one of bearing light and witness to a world that is lost in the darkness of sin (5:8–21). God's children, amazingly, are invited to reflect the light of Jesus Christ to a watching world (vv. 8–17). Christians do this by both living lives of holy obedience and truthfully exposing the dark realities of sin as they witness to God's pure Word. The beloved children of God also shine the light of Jesus the more they are filled with the Holy Spirit, are weaned from worldly sins and desires, give thanks to God, and humbly submit to one another out of love for their Savior (vv. 18–21).

Read Ephesians 5:1–21.

GETTING STARTED

1. In what ways did you seek to imitate your parents, or others whom you admired, as you were growing up? If you have children, in what ways have you seen them seek to imitate you—for better or for worse?

2. Why are church scandals so devastating to our Christian witness? What are some of the things that unconfessed sin and hypocrisy in the Christian community can cause people to think about Christianity and the gospel?

The Fragrance of the Savior, pg. 238
Imitating God means imitating his Son, and that means doing whatever is required to make our lives a fragrant offering and sacrifice to God. The smell of Jesus, the fragrance of the Savior that we are to have waft from our lives, also includes offering and sacrifice.

OBSERVING THE TEXT

3. In what way can you see Ephesians 5:1–2 serving as a kind of "theme passage" for this section? What makes the foundational truths that Paul affirms in these verses so important to an understanding of the commands and warnings in the verses that follow?

4. In what ways does Paul call attention throughout this passage to the importance of believers' *words*—both to the maintaining of purity and to the promoting of good Christian witness?

5. How does Paul call the Ephesian believers to relate to *one another* in this passage? What are some of the ways in which he calls them to relate to the *unbelieving world*?

UNDERSTANDING THE TEXT

6. As Paul warns against sexual impurity in the opening verses of this passage, what different ways of participating in impurity does he address (5:3–5)? Why do you think he connects "covetousness" with sexual immorality and sin (vv. 3, 5)?

7. According to Ephesians 5:6–7, what roles do friendships, partnerships, and words play in a Christian's attempts to maintain purity? Why might Paul see a need to warn believers in the context of this Ephesian church about certain relationships and partnerships?

8. What does Paul say to remind the Ephesians of the new identity they have in Christ, which is the foundation for the commands he gives them (5:8–10)? What are his pictures of "light" and "darkness" meant to represent for his readers? What makes these images a helpful means of summarizing his commands and warnings?

9. How are Christians called to respond to the works and words of "darkness" that they see around them (5:11–14)? Why is it so important for followers of Jesus to use discernment as they seek to "expose" sinful ways of thinking, living, and speaking? In what ways could we "expose" the works and thoughts of darkness—and what is the foundation for our ability to do so?

Danger Ahead, pg. 244
Though we gain strength for the Christian life by savoring our purity and savoring our identity, we ultimately must face the dangers of sin. If we do not recognize the danger, then we are not prepared to live the holy lives God desires. Thus the final dimension of Paul's exhortation against impurity is warning!

10. In what ways do verses 15–20 present a *positive* picture of life in the Spirit—one that contrasts with a life that is lived in darkness and sin? What are some of the characteristics of this kind of life, according to Paul?

11. How are Christians called to relate to one another within the body of Christ, according to Ephesians 5:21? In what way does this verse again call the Ephesian believers' focus back to the foundation of the gospel of Jesus Christ that underlies all of these commands?

BIBLE CONNECTIONS

12. Read 1 John 1:5–7. How does John use the imagery of "light" and "darkness" in these verses—and what truths is he seeking to teach to his audience? In what ways is Paul's use of "light" and "darkness" in Ephesians 5 similar to—and different from—John's use of them?

13. Colossians 3:16–17 is another passage in which Paul instructs Christians to engage in "psalms and hymns and spiritual songs"; and he commands them in that passage to have an attitude of "thankfulness"

to God in their hearts as well. How is singing meant to cultivate an attitude of thankfulness in our hearts—as well as to help us to strengthen ourselves together, as God's people, as we walk with him?

THEOLOGY CONNECTIONS

14. According to answer 32 of the Heidelberg Catechism, a Christian is called a "Christian" for this reason: "that I may confess His Name, present myself a living sacrifice of thankfulness to Him, and with a free and good conscience fight against sin and the devil in this life." What themes from Ephesians 5:1–21 do you see in this answer? What connection does an attitude of thankfulness have to the fight against sin and Satan that following Jesus Christ involves?

15. In Ephesians 5:1–2, Paul presents the *indicative* reality of the gospel (that "Christ loved us and gave himself up for us") before going on to give the *imperative* commands regarding gospel obedience that the rest of the passage contains. What theological errors do we avoid by ensuring that a gospel indicative always precedes any imperatives in our lives?

APPLYING THE TEXT

16. Take some time today to evaluate the purity of your *words* and your *speech*, in light of this passage you have been studying. Are there ways in which you can more intentionally pursue purity—truth, love, and contentment, as well as sexual purity—within your speech?

17. In what ways could you, as well as the Christians in your community, more intentionally seek to "expose" the works and thought patterns of darkness that exist in the world around you (5:11)? What could you do to help this exposure to be loving and gracious instead of angry or argumentative?

18. As you use Ephesians 5:19–21 to consider what a life marked by the Spirit should look like, what areas of your own life show the most need for growth? In particular, how can you grow in the way that you relate to the Christians around you?

The Aim, Object, and Goal, 262

Only when the integration point of our faith is knowing and living out the fullness of the person of Jesus Christ will his person and witness be the true preoccupations that fill our lives. Right doing and thinking are necessary for this proper filling, but Christ alone is the aim, the object, and the goal of what we do and think.

PRAYER PROMPT

As Christians who are "beloved children" of God, we have a gracious invitation from our Savior to humbly imitate him (5:1–2). Today, pray that you would seek to imitate Christ more and more—and not out of joyless obligation but as an act of thankful and free worship. Ask God to expose areas of darkness in your life through the light of the gospel, which has opened your heart to faith in Jesus. Pray that he would enable you to lovingly expose the ways of darkness that exist in the world around you so that you may shine the light of your Savior within the church and to your surrounding community.

LESSON 12

SACRIFICIAL HEAD; SUBMISSIVE WIFE

Ephesians 5:22–33

THE BIG PICTURE

As Paul continues calling the Ephesian believers to be "imitators" of Christ, as God's "beloved children," he turns his focus in this lesson's passage toward the home. The gospel of Jesus Christ must fundamentally shape what is the closest human relationship that many Christians know: the relationship they have with their spouses. Paul first addresses Christian wives and calls them to "submit" to their husbands as the church of God submits to Jesus Christ, who is the "head" of the church (5:22–24). This call to submission is not a call to mindless obedience or weak servility; it is a call for each wife to respect her husband's God-given role of being the spiritual leader—the "head"—of the marriage and home. As Christian wives commit to doing this, they are honoring their Savior and trusting his ultimate and perfect rule over their hearts and lives. For husbands, Paul has quite a lot more to say: he calls them to a role of spiritual headship that is characterized by selfless love, sacrifice, and service (5:25–33). Theirs is a role shaped and defined by Jesus's sacrificial love for his people, which is demonstrated by his death on the cross and his tender, sanctifying love and care of them. Paul concludes this passage with the stunning truth that Christian marriage has the God-given purpose of demonstrating before the world the relationship between Christ and the church (vv. 31–32)!

Christian marriage, then, becomes a testimony to the gospel of Jesus Christ, as wives (through their *submission*) and husbands (through their *sacrifice*) put the beauty of the gospel on display before both each other and a watching world.

Read Ephesians 5:22–33.

GETTING STARTED

1. In our culture today, what makes some people bristle when the word *submit* is used in relation to wives in their marriages? What mistake might some people make when they interpret what the Bible means by that word?

2. In what ways can male headship be abused in a marriage? Why is it so important for us to think *biblically* about this concept rather than to embrace our culture's idea of patriarchy?

A Sacred Love, pg. 288

The whole notion of the church as both Christ's body and bride is mirrored in the one-flesh relationship between a husband and his bride. The mystery then is how Christ, through the gospel, calls a bride to himself, and how Christian marriage is to illustrate this great sacred act. For this husband, this ultimately means that a husband's love for his wife is intimately tied to his knowledge of Christ's love for us.

OBSERVING THE TEXT

3. What do you notice about the comparative length of the sections of teaching that Paul gives to wives and then to husbands? Bearing in mind that he was writing within a patriarchal context that often downplayed the value of women, why might he have done this? What might he be attempting to communicate to Christians about the way in which the gospel transforms a husband's view of, and behavior toward, his wife?

4. What connections does Paul make between his commands to both wives and husbands and their relationship with Jesus Christ? In what ways do his instructions regarding marriage flow directly from gospel truths?

5. While wives are called to "submit" to their husbands, who have the role of the "head" in the marriage, how is this role of the husband described—and after what is it modeled? If a husband truly loves and serves his wife in the way that this passage commands, how could it help her submission to him to be joyful and natural?

UNDERSTANDING THE TEXT

6. What connection does Paul draw between a wife's relationship with Jesus Christ and her submission to her husband (5:22)? Since submission does not mean mindless obedience (and certainly does not mean partnering in sin), what *does* it mean for a Christian wife?

7. What relationship does Paul say serves as the model for the relationship between wives and husbands (5:23–24)? In what way can this picture be helpful for Christian wives as they seek to apply what these verses say to their marriages?

8. How does Paul describe the *kind* of loving headship that Christian husbands must provide for their wives (5:25)? Why is it important for the cross of Jesus Christ to serve as the primary picture of the way in which husbands are to love their wives as they fulfill the role of the sacrificial head of the marriage?

Husbanding by Sacrifice, pg. 286
This is the leadership of humility, the headship of service—husbanding by sacrifice. To it God calls men who would be biblical heads of their homes. A Christian husband leads by service. He heads his family through selfless love. He has the primary biblical responsibility in the home to set a spiritual standard by his own sacrifice to make God's grace evident.

9. What is Jesus's ultimate and eternal goal for his beloved bride—the church (5:26–27)? In what way should his desire for the church to be sanctified and presented to him for eternity shape husbands' own ultimate desires, hopes, and prayers for their wives?

10. In 5:28–30, Paul describes the way in which Jesus Christ lovingly and tenderly nourishes and cares for the church, as if it were his own body. In what way should these verses shape and inform the way that Christian husbands love their wives? How do they rule out domineering or abusive behavior within a marriage altogether?

11. What is marriage ultimately about, according to Paul (5:31–32)? When husbands *love* their wives as Christ loves the church, and when wives *respect* their husbands out of reverence for Christ (5:33), in what way can this display the truth of the gospel to the world?

BIBLE CONNECTIONS

12. Read Genesis 2:18–25—the passage from which Paul quotes in this lesson's reading. What do you notice about the original intention that God had for man and woman when they are together in marriage? What is beautiful about this passage—and what do you learn from it about the heart that God has for his people?

13. In 1 Peter 3:1–2, Peter offers some teaching specifically for Christian wives who are joined with unbelieving husbands. How does he instruct them to live within their marriages? What should be their goal, and what should they pray for, as they submit to and love their husbands?

THEOLOGY CONNECTIONS

14. The Westminster Larger Catechism explains, in answer 139, that the seventh commandment calls God's people to avoid "undue delay of marriage; having more wives or husbands than one at the same time; unjust divorce, or desertion; idleness, gluttony, drunkenness, unchaste company ... and all other provocations to, or acts of uncleanness, either in ourselves or others." In what way should the high, Christ-exalting view of marriage that Paul offers us in Ephesians 5:22–33 motivate us to be faithful within the context of marriage—and pure outside it?

15. Jesus is clear that in the new heavens and new earth, men and women will neither "marry nor [be] given in marriage" (Matt. 22:30). How can the temporary nature of human marriage serve as a reminder to married men and women that their responsibility to their spouses echoes into eternity? Why is it so important to encourage them to put their *eternal* spouse—Jesus Christ—first in their hearts and minds?

APPLYING THE TEXT

16. If you are not married, how can the truths of the gospel that are reflected in this passage, as well as the beautiful intention God has for husbands and wives through their marriages, still encourage you?

17. If you are married, what aspects of this passage does your marriage reflect most weakly? What steps might you take in order to humbly, and perhaps with repentance, seek to live out Paul's commands, so that your marriage may display the relationship between Christ and his church more beautifully?

18. Husbands, in what way could meditating on the sacrifice that Jesus made for *you* help you to be more joyfully willing to sacrifice for your wife? Wives, how might deepening your love for Christ and your trust in his headship enable you to submit joyfully to your husband—as imperfect as he is?

PRAYER PROMPT

As you close your study of this remarkable passage, pray first that God would move your heart to worship him as you consider the beauty of the gospel that is on display in it (whether you are married or not!). Thank your Savior for giving himself in your place, and praise him for the fact that he will one day "present" the church to himself, in splendor, as his spotless bride (5:27). If you are married, ask God to help you more joyfully, humbly, and worshipfully obey the commands that Paul gives in this passage—whether that involves submission (for wives) or sacrificial headship (for husbands). Pray that, as you do this, the beauty of the gospel will emanate from your marriage—to the glory of your Savior.

A Balanced Construction, pg. 295

The requirement to use one's gifts to glorify another becomes most apparent when we recognize the balanced construction of the instruction Paul gives wives *and* husbands in this passage. Paul instructs husbands to use their headship as Christ used his for the glory of his bride, the church. . . . At the same time wives are told not to disregard submission so that they rob their husbands of "respect."

LESSON 13

GOD'S HOUSEHOLD AND GOD'S ARMOR

Ephesians 6:1–24

THE BIG PICTURE

Paul has just given his readers a beautiful, Christ-exalting vision regarding Christian marriage: wives who *submit* to their husbands in the way that the church submits to Christ, and husbands who *serve* their wives as the sacrificial heads of their marriages, according to the pattern of Christ. Now his commands reach further into the Christian household, as he demonstrates how the reality of the gospel should shape not only the marriage relationship but also other, authority-based relationships in that sphere. First he addresses parents and children, calling children to exhibit God-honoring obedience and fathers to apply loving discipline, instruction, and nurture in the Lord (6:1–4). Next he turns to the relationship between masters and bondservants—who would have, in most cases, been considered in the society of these Ephesian believers to be part of the ancient "household" arrangement (6:5–9). Christian masters are not to rule through abuse, violence, or anger; their behavior must be shaped more and more by their "Master" in heaven (v. 9). Bondservants are called to display sincere obedience and respect, since they ultimately view their work and service as worship of their Savior, Jesus Christ (vv. 5–6).

As Paul then concludes his letter to the Ephesians, he seeks to instruct and equip the Ephesian believers in a more general way regarding their lives of spiritual warfare—to leave them armed by God and equipped to engage a sinful world for the glory of their Savior (6:10–20). Using military metaphors, he commands them to prepare for Christian engagement using spiritual weapons—God's Word, God's Spirit, and God's gospel. Such teaching reminds us that our battle in this world is ultimately spiritual—and thus that our equipping must be spiritual as well. Paul concludes, finally, with personal words of both greeting and blessing for the Ephesian believers (6:21–24).

Read Ephesians 6:1–24.

GETTING STARTED

1. What dangers result when Christians' public life (or "church life") is different from the life they live at home with those who are closest to them? Why is it so important for the gospel of Jesus Christ to permeate our household and family relationships?

2. What misunderstandings have Christians sometimes had regarding the *kind* of battle, or warfare, that they are to wage in this world for the sake of Christ? What dangers result when we fail to understand that we are engaged in a *spiritual* battle and serve a Savior whose kingdom is not of this world?

OBSERVING THE TEXT

3. Even throughout the many commands Paul issues in this passage regarding the Ephesians' horizontal relationships (those that they have with other people), in what way does he also continually point their eyes upward to their *vertical* relationship with Christ?

4. What countercultural commands does Paul issue to people in positions of *authority* in the first nine verses of this chapter? How might these commands have challenged the way that people with power functioned in their homes and places of work?

5. What are your observations about the kinds of weapons and spiritual equipment that Paul urges Christians to take up (6:10–20)? What do those observations tell you about the *way* that he wants the Ephesian believers to engage with the world around them, as well as the type of *war* that he wants them to fight, for Jesus's glory?

Authority That Reflects the Savior, pg. 326

The complexities of properly exercising authority in the Christian home and workplace drive us back to consideration of the foundations and purposes of all authority in the home. The way the apostle structures his presentation of these issues makes it clear that all expressions of authority . . . are to reflect the character of the Savior. . . . By using our authority for the good of others we discover our own most noble purposes and are drawn most closely to the divine nature.

UNDERSTANDING THE TEXT

6. What clear command does Paul give to Christian children in 6:1–3, and in what way does he ground it in God's law? What does verse 4 call fathers to avoid as they raise their children, and what are they (as well as *all* Christian parents) specifically called to do?

7. The commands that Paul issues to Christian bondservants are grounded in their fundamental identity in Christ. (Note: the "bondservants" or "slaves" who are mentioned here could have belonged to ancient households in a variety of ways and for different reasons or amounts of time.) In what way does Paul say that such bondservants' service and worship of Jesus should affect their service of their earthly masters?

8. What warnings does Paul give to earthly masters in 6:9? What eternal truths are to shape the way they treat anyone over whom they have authority? What application could this have for Christian leaders today?

9. How does Paul characterize the fundamental nature of the battle and struggle that Christians wage in this world (6:10–12)? Why is it important for us to remember that our fight is not fundamentally against *people*

who do not know Christ but against Satan, sin, and the powers of darkness? How should a realization of this shape our gospel ministry—as well as our treatment of unbelievers?

10. What are believers to arm themselves with, according to Ephesians 6:13–18? How does the military metaphor that Paul uses help us to understand the spiritual battle we are engaged in as followers of Jesus Christ in a sinful world? What example does Paul himself provide of how to wage spiritual warfare for the glory of Jesus Christ (6:19–20)?

11. How does Paul seek to encourage the Ephesian believers as he closes his letter (6:21–22)? What words of blessing does he leave them with—and how does he point them to the centrality of Christ and his gospel yet again (6:23–24)?

The Love We Require and the Love We Must Give, pg. 326
Under what is sometimes intense pressure and pain, we are to lift those in our care to the Lord. By the ways we model the Lord and mold others' perception of him, we discern the love we require as well as the love we must give. By lifting others to the Savior we become like him, and thus discover more of the love of the Savior who lifts us to heaven by his sacrifice.

BIBLE CONNECTIONS

12. Read Philemon 10–16, and note the instructions Paul gives to Philemon regarding how he should receive his former slave Onesimus, who is now a believer, back into his household. How does this passage demonstrate that slavery is ultimately incompatible with gospel Christianity? In what way do Paul's commands to Philemon urge him to undergo a fundamental shift in the way he views his former slave, since they are now equal in Christ?

13. In 1 Peter 5:6–9, the apostle Peter describes the way that our "adversary," Satan, "prowls around" and attempts to attack the children of God. Read those verses now. In what way does Peter's description of Satan's malicious activity demonstrate the need for us to arm ourselves spiritually, as Paul describes in Ephesians 6:10–18?

THEOLOGY CONNECTIONS

14. Answer 64 of the Westminster Shorter Catechism explains that the fifth commandment, along with telling Christians to honor their fathers and mothers, offers broader implications as well, regarding their calling in the areas of "preserving the honor, and performing the duties, belonging to every one in their several places and relations, as superiors, inferiors, or equals." What evidence do you see of these broader principles in the passage you have been studying in this lesson—and especially in

6:1–9? To what other types of relationships might these principles be applied?

15. In his commentary, Bryan Chapell writes of Martin Luther's spiritual battles with the devil—which once led him to hurl his inkwell at him when he sensed his presence in his study![1] What does this remind us about the unseen spiritual world? What should be the root of our confidence as we live for Jesus and withstand the schemes of Satan?

APPLYING THE TEXT

16. If you are still in your parents' home and under their authority, what influence should this passage have on the way you live with them as a follower of Jesus Christ? And if you are a parent, what could you do to further your commitment not to "provoke" your children and instead to lovingly instruct them in the Lord (6:4)?

17. In the context of your positions of authority (whether you are a parent, a boss, a teacher, or some other authority), in what ways could you

1. See Bryan Chapell, *Ephesians* (Phillipsburg, NJ: P&R Publishing, 2009), 327.

more lovingly obey the commands that are given to masters in this passage? How should your worship of your perfect Master in heaven better shape the way you lead those who are under your care?

18. What steps can you take to put on the "armor of God" in the weeks and months that are ahead (6:11)? How does your personal time with God equip you for this battle? What contribution does the church of God have to your being equipped with proper spiritual armor?

PRAYER PROMPT

As you complete both your study of this lesson and your study of Paul's letter to the Ephesians, praise God for the glorious hope of the gospel and for the family into which he has welcomed you through your faith in Christ. Ask him to give you the strength and power, by his Spirit, to allow the relationships in your household to be shaped more and more by your Master's rule in your heart. Pray that your God would arm you with his Word, Spirit, and salvation so that you may engage in courageous gospel witness, for his glory, in order that others might come to know the Savior, too.

Equipped for Spiritual Warfare, pg. 329

Paul equips us for spiritual warfare. He assures us that we can stand against the Devil's schemes. . . . There is hope of spiritual victory over our compulsions when we use the apostle's instruction to understand the nature of our enabling, our Adversary, our weaponry, and Christ's empowering love.

Jon Nielson is senior pastor of Spring Valley Presbyterian Church in Roselle, Illinois, and the author of *Bible Study: A Student's Guide*, among other books. He has served in pastoral positions at Holy Trinity Church, Chicago, and College Church, Wheaton, Illinois, and as director of training for the Charles Simeon Trust.

Bryan Chapell (MDiv, Covenant Theological Seminary; PhD, Southern Illinois University) is stated clerk *pro tempore* of the Presbyterian Church in America. He is senior pastor emeritus of Grace Presbyterian Church, president emeritus of Covenant Theological Seminary in St. Louis, general editor of *The ESV Gospel Transformation Bible*, and a respected author.

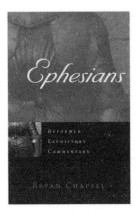

Bryan Chapell, noted preacher and teacher of preaching, unfolds Paul's glorious description of how the triumph of the church will occur and what our roles are in Christ's ultimate victory. When we lift our eyes beyond personal borders to share even a glimpse of Paul's expansive vision, then we, too, will join his doxology for God's amazing grace that saves individuals, empowers the church, and, through both, transforms the world.

The Reformed Expository Commentary (REC) series is accessible to both pastors and lay readers. Each volume in the series provides exposition that gives careful attention to the biblical text, is doctrinally Reformed, focuses on Christ through the lens of redemptive history, and applies the Bible to our contemporary setting.

Praise for the Reformed Expository Commentary Series

"Well-researched and well-reasoned, practical and pastoral, shrewd, solid, and searching." —**J. I. Packer**

"A rare combination of biblical insight, theological substance, and pastoral application." —**Al Mohler**

"Here, rigorous expository methodology, nuanced biblical theology, and pastoral passion combine." —**R. Kent Hughes**

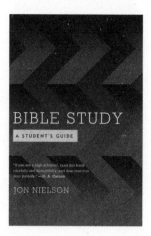

Have you ever been to a "Bible study" that didn't have much "Bible" or "study" at all? Without a proper understanding of how to do it, students can be disappointed or scared away from studying the Bible. So what is Bible study—and can it work for high schoolers?

No stranger to teaching the Bible to teenagers, Jon Nielson confirms that real, meaningful Bible study is not only possible for students but important. He takes students seriously and expects them to take their faith seriously. Unpacking five truths about the Bible—that it is God speaking, is powerful, is understandable, is literary, and is one story—he demonstrates how the Bible should be studied and how teenagers themselves can lead that study.

"If you are a high schooler, read this book carefully and thoughtfully, and then loan it to your parents. Chances are pretty good that they'll benefit from it as much as you will."
—**D. A. Carson**, Editor, Pillar New Testament Commentary series